Brown Davis Interiors | Photograph by Moris Moreno Photography

Fanny Haim & Associates | Photograph by Carlos Domenech Photography

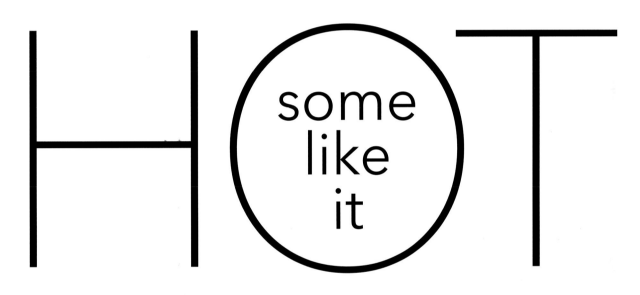

HOT
some like it

inspiring spaces
by florida's hottest designers

Beth Benton Buckley

Published by

benton **buckley books**
be bold.

www.bentonbuckleybooks.com

Principal Publisher: Beth Buckley
Associate Publisher: Sheri Lazenby
Lead Writer: Lindsey Wilson
Contributing Writer: Sam Boykin
Editor: Rosalie Wilson
Lead Graphics: Morganne Stewart
Production Manager/Graphics: Erica Core

FIRST EDITION

Distributed by Independent Publishers Group
800.888.4741

PUBLISHER'S DATA

Some Like It HOT
Inspiring Spaces By Florida's Hottest Designers

Library of Congress Cataloging-in-Publication Data
has been applied for.
ISBN: 978-0-9994818-0-6

For information about custom editions, special sales, or premium and
corporate books, please contact benton buckley books at bebold@
bentonbuckleybooks.com.

Dust Jacket Front:
Interior Design: Sharron Lannan | Photo: Troy Campbell Studio
Dust Jacket Inside Front Flap:
Interior Design: Juan Carlos Arcila-Duque | Photo: Troy Campbell Studio

First Printing 2018
10 9 8 7 6 5 4 3 2 1

Phil Kean Design Group | Photograph by Uneek Photography

designers

amy herman

amy kelly

anil kakar

brianna michelle

david l. smith

deborah wecselman

debra butler

eve glass beres

fanny haim

hillary littlejohn scurtis

jennifer garrigues

jonathan parks

juan carlos arcila-duque

juan poggi

judith liegeois

kurt dannwolf & lachmee chin

laura martzell

leili fatemi

margarita & cristina courtney

pamela iannacio

phil kean

robert brown & todd davis

robert rionda

robert zemnickis

sandra diaz-velasco

sam robin

sarah zohar

sharron lannan

susan lovelace

whitney bloom

In today's social media-drenched world, images—no matter how beautiful—are fleeting. Inspiration pops up for a second and then is gone, lost in the nonstop commotion of information overload. Design, however, is something that lives with you, that you surround yourself with daily and that influences your thoughts, emotions, and well-being. To find and be able to hold onto an image that provokes inspiration could, potentially, change your entire life.

I consider the process of gathering these remarkable artists adorning the pages of *Some Like It HOT* akin to curating a gallery. With each internationally recognized designer who fills our pages, we expand and deepen their reach. There is no greater pleasure in what I do than to seek out the most sought-after, revered, and acclaimed designers, as well as yet-discovered talent in this permanent collection. It is awe-inspiring to see such diversity and talent in one compilation, and even more amazing to realize their work and philosophies will exist to spark creativity and inspiration in you, our readers.

Florida's style is as unique as the people who travel from all across the world to visit or live here. Tastes and preferences change as you move throughout the state, but there is always an invigorating sense of excitement to the environments these designers create. This artistic destination is a place of inspiration to designers, and those who want to be inspired. People from coast to coast look to this eclectic locale to see what's hot and happening, and whether you live in California or Maine, you will surely find something in this collection—a rug, a piece of artwork, a color palette, an idea—to take with you and use in your own home.

The 30 incredible designers featured in this book are tastemakers, not only for Floridians but for around the world. While the pages that adorn the book are of Florida residences, the work of the designers spans the globe. It is this diversity that ensures everyone will be able to glean their own inspiration from the designs presented here, and be able to peruse the pages again and again to find new ideas.

I often repeat the Roman philosopher Cicero's thought that "a room without books is like a body without a soul." Assembling this group of inspiring and accomplished designers into a coffee-table book has ensured that their creative souls will remain to ignite a passion for beautiful interiors and magnificent viewpoints for many years to come.

Beth Buckley

Eolo A&I Design | Photograph by Juan Pablo Estupinan

Robert Rionda Interiors | Photograph by Troy Campbell Studio

"By wisdom a house is built, and through understanding, it is established;

through knowledge its rooms are filled
with rare and beautiful treasures."

Proverb

AMY HERMAN

AS AN ACCOMPLISHED PAINTER AND PHOTOGRAPHER, Amy Herman is exceptionally sensitive to composition and color. Her interior design work reflects her curatorial eye—she is able to work in practically any genre, adapting a design's style and theme to perfectly suit each client who seeks her assistance.

"I like to joke that I am somewhat of a savant when it comes to art and design," says Amy. "I was born with the gift of being able to retain anything visual. Photographic memory is a powerful tool for creativity."

She channels that creativity into design projects—and fine artwork, as she is "always creating, painting, sculpting, designing products, and buying art supplies"—that have been lauded by multiple publications and enjoyed by both private and commercial clientele. Aided at her firm, Amy Herman Interiors, by a top-notch team of architects, engineers, and contractors, she handles all aspects of design and construction with ease, relishing the art of collaboration with industry professionals as well as with her clients.

With a degree in design from the University of Miami as her base, Amy expertly utilizes what she views as the indispensable tools of her trade: longevity, balance, flow, the ability to edit and curate, and insane amounts of passion.

"I continually have people say to me, 'I wish I had your job. It seems like so much fun!' My job is fun, but the design business is a serious one," she explains. "I think it surprises people how detailed and demanding a profession it is."

That all-important attention to detail goes hand in hand with timing and trust, two vital elements of her career that may not always remain top of mind for her clients, but which Amy never overlooks. It takes an enormous amount of trust for people to surrender their personal spaces to someone else, but Amy is diligent about remaining true to their vision while guiding their style with her proven expertise.

One of her tried and true principals is the "two-week rule," which operates under the belief that it takes roughly two weeks for someone to acclimate to and accept his or her new surroundings. By encouraging her clients to always keep the rule in mind, she has found that many are more receptive to new ideas, and more inclined to take design risks that end up reaping continual rewards.›

"Design is not implementing a certain style; it's a curation and a collaboration."

To help keep her own creativity stimulated, Amy seeks out inspiration through travel—visiting her daughter in New York City is a particular favorite trip—admiring the work of other designers, and, of course, art. In turn, this allows her to produce fabulous turn-key projects, many concentrated within the realm of residential new construction but some which also include renovation, that consistently delight homeowners. The importance of following one's passion has led, in Amy's case, to a fulfilling career that brings joy to others through their everyday spaces.

AMY KELLY

GROWING UP IN THE FLORIDA PANHANDLE, AMY KELLY would often tag along with her dad, a property developer, as he met with various clients and city officials. "I was always fascinated with his blueprints," she says. "I would open them up and study them for hours."

This fascination with design continued into her teenage years. Allowances came in the form of decorating her bedroom at 13, a childhood highlight that eventually paved her path into college. She attended Florida State University and graduated from the Visual Communications program with a bachelor's degree in interior design. Next, Amy spent a year in Florence, Italy, earning a master's in interior and product design from Accademia Italiana. Her time abroad was not purely academic though, as she recalls the experience had a profound impact on her life.

"Feeling connected to the culture, architecture, and history of Italy led me to travel back several times," she says. "I often dream about Italy and it will hold a piece of my heart forever."

When Amy's time in Florence came to an end, she returned home amidst the Great Recession. Struggling to find a job, she made the brave decision to move to South Florida and explore the industry. She worked with a variety of designers, and as fate brought her back home, she finally found her match with Janet Taylor, founder of Janet Taylor Interiors. Amy started with Janet as an assistant, and after years of dedication, eventually became a partner to Taylor & Kelly Interiors. As Janet imagined her path to retirement, the transition to Amy's own design studio came naturally.

Nestled among the beaches of South Walton, off the 30A corridor, lies Amy's beautiful design studio—Kelly Collective Interiors. The intimate company is a full-service interior design firm that specializes in high-end residential projects including personal residences, vacation homes and investment properties.

Amy describes her design style as "natural coastal elegance." Imagine an aesthetic consisting of natural light and colors inspired by Florida's many green trees, mesmerizing blue waters, and breathtaking orange sunsets. She also incorporates natural textures and materials into her designs, such as linen, seagrass, rattan, bamboo, reclaimed woods, and oyster shells. "Bringing the outdoors in creates a compelling and fluid space between the interior and exterior, which is important in Florida," she says.

She stresses that she learns something new with every design project, as she's constantly dealing with unique challenges and situations. And contrary to what some people may believe, being a great interior designer goes far beyond "pillows and paint," she says. "You also need to be educated about the history of design, the structural integrity of buildings, building codes, spatial concepts, ethics, psychology, and much more."›

> "Bringing the outdoors in creates a compelling and fluid space between the interior and exterior, which is important in Florida."

It's crucial to focus on the details of each project, whether it's a small renovation or a complete house design. When the project is completed, a well-designed home should be harmonious with the exterior environment, while reflecting the personality of the clients and maintaining a timeless, functional, and livable feel-good atmosphere. During her career Amy says she's learned that things don't have to be perfect to be beautiful.

ANIL KAKAR

Photographs by Kris Tamburello

JUST AS HIS WORLD TRAVELS HAVE BEEN FAR-REACHING and varied, so has the route Anil Kakar took to opening Interiors by Kakar House of Design. The acclaimed designer was born in New Delhi, India, and spent several years of his early childhood there before moving with his family to Michigan, where he stayed to earn his bachelor's degree from Michigan State University. From there it was on to a prominent design firm in Chicago, which eventually led him to South Florida, where he combined his passion for design and business by earning his MBA from the University of Miami.

But while working as a wealth advisor for several major banks, Anil just couldn't shake his desire to create. After completing several personal projects and at the urging of friends, he decided to pursue design full-time.

"I strive to create beautiful and comfortable spaces that will enhance my clients' lifestyle for years to come," says Anil. "Something that is completely in keeping with their vision and their lifestyle, while infusing it with my creative talents."

Anil founded B11 Design in 2010, naming his eventual empire's parent company in honor of his paternal grandparents' house number in New Delhi. Kakar House of Design, Anil's retail store—where avid shoppers can find stunning furniture, lighting, sculpture, rugs, and accessories—followed two short years later.

That same urge to source incredible décor from all over the world for his store also fuels Anil's designs, which include not only residential and corporate but also retail, hospitality, and even private jets.

"I use eclectic pieces, from art to fabrics to furnishings to lighting, in each project, to create that unique vision," he says. "From antiques to vintage to custom and new, we design for a life well lived and well-traveled."

Treating each space as "a visual escape," Anil layers his creativity, time, energy, and talent until the resulting design is reflective of his clients' wishes. And he's not afraid to do the heavy lifting himself, if that's what it takes to get a room just right.

"A truly great designer will really get in there and do whatever is necessary to get the job done, even if that means lifting furniture and dusting and cleaning a bit," he says. "I don't just delegate—I really do whatever needs to be done myself. Nothing is too menial for me, or any good designer worth their salt."

Anil also understands the importance of timelines, and how many of his clients find it difficult to remain patient when it comes to experiencing the final reveal of their new space: a room (or several) that they will live in and love for years to come. He's a problem-solver and a doer, and maintains an easy rhythm throughout the entire length of each project. Even unexpected challenges have taught Anil to stop and seek inspiration from places both expected and unlikely, and he does so often on his adventurous travels. ›

"No two designs are ever alike, nor should they be. Each is a personal stamp of the people inhabiting those spaces."

"I am always inspired by Mother Nature," Anil says. "She is the greatest designer, with all the colors, patterns, and textures. When I am traveling, I feel greatly inspired by past civilizations and current cultures and societies."

BRIANNA MICHELLE

BRIANNA MICHELLE HAS BEEN AN INTERIOR DESIGNER her entire life, even before she knew it was a profession. From an early age, she remembers having an inexplicable understanding of architecture, space planning, and design. When other kids were drawing cars and airplanes, Brianna was busy sketching floorplans and elevations.

She originally thought that she might want to be an architect, as she gained inspiration from walking custom homes that her contractor grandfather was building. But when Brianna was in high school, her aunt mailed her an article from The New York Times, titled "The Profession of Interior Design." Before that point, she had never even heard of interior design. "The article really put a name to what I wanted to do. It seemed like the perfect fit," says Brianna.

That article set Brianna on a path to pursuing her passion of design at Michigan State University. Four years later she graduated Cum Laude with a Bachelor of Arts in Interior Design. Immediately following graduation, she accepted her first position as a design assistant at a firm in the much warmer climate of Florida.

Using the work ethic instilled in her by her parents, she earned her state license and over the next seven years climbed her way up the design industry ladder. In 2010, she took a leap of faith and opened Brianna Michelle Interior Design in Winter Park, Fl. This was not an easy decision for Brianna, as she knew having a successful business was much easier said than done.

"It was a great opportunity to open my own business, but I'm not a huge risk taker," she says. "I knew I had the right experience and industry relationships before I jumped in, but it was still a frightening move."

Now, Brianna and her team at BMID, who specialize in new construction, renovations, and commercial environments, provide turnkey design services on 12-15 projects a year ranging in size from 5,000 to 12,000 square feet. They have successfully completed projects from coast to coast within the U.S. and are currently exploring overseas opportunities.

While Brianna says her design style is generally modern with a classic, timeless aesthetic, she says each project's overall look is determined by the client. "The world of design is all about understanding people," she says. "I always want to keep things fresh and original, but it has to relate to the client's lifestyle. So much of what we do is about how people live and interact within a space.">

"The world of design is all about understanding people. I always want to keep things fresh and original, but it has to relate to the client's lifestyle. So much of what we do is about how people live and interact within a space."

Right around the time Brianna launched her business, she met her future husband, Ryan, who happens to be a builder, as fate would have it. The two married in 2014 and they've since worked on several projects together. They also designed and built their personal home in Maitland, where they welcomed their son, Ryker. "My husband and I work really well as a team," she says. "We met at a point in our lives when we both had career goals and were determined to make them happen. We're now making them happen together."

DAVID L. SMITH

BEING LOCATED IN THE FLORIDA KEYS HAS CERTAINLY influenced David L. Smith's aesthetic: tropical and approachable, or "barefoot modern," as he calls it. But always stylish too, as the seasoned buyer, importer, and designer has learned to remain timeless with his work, mixing saturated colors with natural materials and woods to create his signature look.

"I always want to ensure my choices will still be relevant years down the road," he says. "Working with a broad range of clients allows me to explore and experience style in different ways, so the definition is always evolving."

David has built his company on the principle of always incorporating the needs and wishes of his clients, but presenting the final product in an unexpected way. He gathers inspiration from his travels—he's always anticipating which spot on the map he'll visit next—and is constantly on the lookout for unlikely catalysts.

"When I find a pleasing aesthetic, I try to take it apart and understand why it works," says David. "What the balance or imbalance is offering, or how a juxtaposition can hold my attention. I especially like inspiration that isn't obvious, but forces you to discover its magic."

That discovery requires a healthy dose of patience—an incredibly important attribute to exercise throughout the process of interior design. David has learned this over the years, and he imparts that hard-earned wisdom to his clients through clear and constant communication. Listening, too, is an invaluable skill. Quality doesn't happen overnight, he has found, and so keeping everyone apprised of each stage is key. Often during a project David will develop an instinct and then stay loyal to it, though he recognizes when it's imperative to change course, be flexible, and bend the rules in order to try something new.

Working both hard and smart has resulted in stunning homes across the Keys, each so impeccably executed that David himself would be proud to live in them.

"Never put out a product that you wouldn't live with personally," he maintains. "If you make a mistake, fix it. Create spaces that everyone can use and enjoy, and feel comfortable occupying."›

"It's important to avoid the cliché and strive for timeless design."

Sometimes ensuring that everything is done to his exacting standards means that David himself is the one picking up a wrench or a paintbrush. It's all part of being flexible and willing to do whatever the moment calls for in order to end up with a beautiful home. "It's important to take risks and find those boundaries that pull you away from the status quo, yet keep you related to your design statement and environment," David says. "Being decisive is perhaps the most important trait an interior designer can possess."

DEBORAH WECSELMAN

WHEN PEEKING INTO A HOME THAT'S IN THE PROCESS of being designed by Deborah Wecselman, it's not unusual to find the designer herself up on a ladder, checking measurements. Or swapping out paint samples, to see how they appear at different times of the day. Or inspecting the seam of a pillow, to make sure it is up to her exacting standards.

That eye for detail and those perfectionist tendencies are part of what make Wecselman and her firm, DWD Inc., so successful. Founded in 2000, DWD has deliberately remained small in order for Deborah and her team to fully commit their energy and attention to each individual project.

"I believe in the final product, and I do not like to veer from it," says Deborah. "It's wise to integrate all elements in a space beforehand, but also to never let budget dictate creativity."

After completing her BFA in environmental design from Parson's School of Design in New York, Deborah—who was born in Lima, Peru—began her career as a design associate in Ralph Lauren's store development department. She quickly moved through the renowned fashion brand's ranks, becoming a senior director of international store design and creating more than 5,000 shops around the globe.

"Though good design never happens without inspiration and imagination, great design celebrates reality as well."

Working with many of the world's finest designers no doubt informed her own eclectic sense of style, but when partnering with clients Deborah instantly gets in sync with them and uses their requests and preferences as her starting point.

A well-designed space is, after all, the creation of a lifestyle, one that reflects people's everyday needs and heartfelt passions. Deborah never forgets that the choices she makes for each room are ones that her clients will be interacting with daily for years to come. With that in mind, DWD's specialty is producing spaces that are classically modern, but with hints of the past that complement contemporary living. And it's vital, Deborah has found, to begin with a good base.

"It's ideal to start with a good architectural envelope," she says, "meaning the floors, walls, and ceilings. From there you can begin to introduce the soft goods: furniture, accessories, and artwork."

It's also important to remember that designing any space is a process, one that will almost surely come with surprises and depends heavily on the people who work on it. As a seasoned designer, Deborah knows with whom to work and how to anticipate any twists, and can soothe her clients when such twists arise.›

"You need to have realistic expectations about budgeting," she cautions, "as well as understand the timing of all the elements necessary to create a design." When she's not wrangling all those elements—and checking on their quality herself—Deborah seeks out inspiration of her own through travel, going antiquing, watching movies, and adding to her impressive magazine collection. "I am obsessed," she admits.

DEBRA BUTLER

THOUGH HER CAREER HAS REVOLVED AROUND design in one way or another since 2006, the outdoors is where Debra Butler feels the most at home. The nature-loving designer enjoys the bountiful fishing, snorkeling, boating, and hiking of the Florida Keys, although those hobbies are sometimes hard to fit in among her numerous design projects.

Debra is endlessly devoted to each project. "I get so excited about projects that I often wake up at two in the morning with a new idea that I capture in a bedside notebook," she says.

Collaborating with her colleagues and local craftspeople, her crystalized ideas are then, most importantly, shared with the clients who have entrusted her with their most sacred space: their home.

Like most designers, Debra eschews her own personal taste—clean, modern, and monochromatic—in order to create a personalized sanctuary that will look stunning while functioning well for those who live in it. But unlike many others, she takes a hands-on approach to each step of a design process or remodel, whether that means discovering just the right piece of furniture at an exclusive showroom or getting down and dirty in the granite yard in order to secure the perfect slab for a countertop.

"It's important to be flexible," she says. "I'm most concerned with creating beautiful living spaces for the people who will live there."

She has her previous businesses to thank for this jack-of-all-trades approach. Debra began by specializing in custom cabinetry before launching a home design and consulting business, All Out Designs, in 2011. By 2012, she was ready to open her current studio, which builds on the cooperative spirit she cultivated with industry professionals and tradespeople.

And now more than ever that synergy includes her clients, with whom Debra establishes close relationships that last throughout the life of their project, and often beyond.

"I always hope to convey to my clients that their job is my favorite job," says Debra. "I put a lot of time and thought into their space. Some projects can take one to two years, so we definitely develop a relationship."

Getting things just right is important to Debra, whether that means mixing the perfect paint hue, coordinating plumbing fixtures, sourcing distinctive accessories, or anything in between. Her own 600-square-foot Key West home, which she describes as "casual, simple, and organized," is getting a loving remodel back to its original 1900s revival feel. The only pops of color among the black, white, and wood come from art she has collected from mostly local artists. Even the yard, with its small garden and refreshing pool, is deliberately easy to maintain for the enjoyment of her and her rescued Boston terrier, Raymond. ›

"It's important to be flexible. I'm most concerned with creating beautiful living spaces for the people who will live there."

Debra has also been rehabbing a 1973 Airstream trailer that lives on a plot of land she owns in western New Mexico, perfecting its original '70s design while introducing modern elements. "I get to go 'glamping' at least once a year," Debra says. "My future plan is to be out there long enough to build a small adobe house off the grid, using all local materials and labor—mostly my own, of course."

EVE GLASS BERES

FOR EVE GLASS BERES, WHEN THE HARMONY OF interior architecture is seamlessly interwoven with the smallest details, the collective vision of her designs take shape. The sculpting of that harmony is the essence of her art.

Eve considers interior spaces to be the canvas of her clients' lives. Collaboration is paramount in the creation process and is at the heart of her inspired designs. Drawing on inspiration and innovation, but mostly a dedication and commitment to excellence and beauty, Eve approaches each new project with the goal of creating a space that truly reflects her clients' vision.

"We are able to co-create these spaces that beautifully support and enrich our clients' lifestyle," she says. "I believe in the authenticity of material, luxurious textiles, and a richly layered, neutral palette, which allows us to create freshly elegant, timeless rooms that are comfortably livable."

Eve's connection to the elegance and grandeur of historical architecture and design began at an early age. By the time she was in college, she had begun to think of design as a beautiful composition, where the many layers lend a supportive role to the creation of the whole.

Traveling the world has allowed Eve to experience myriad architectural styles first-hand.

"My main sources of inspiration come from the historic beauty of Italian architecture, the streamlined design of European midcentury modern, and the glamorous and chic styles of Art Deco and French Moderne," she says.

As a devoted wife and mother of two, Eve has welcomed the challenge of designing an "active" house that's resilient yet beautiful, and perfectly suited for any lifestyle. Her own rule is "purchase only items that you really love, knowing you can always find a home for something that is meaningful." A stylish mix of beautiful things is exciting and interesting, she believes, and certainly more personal.

Working personally with each of her clients over an extended period of time allows Eve a glimpse into their lives. It is the tailoring of each design to the clients' unique desires and lifestyles that really bring the spaces to life.›

> "There is always a way to the solution—you just have to use your creativity to find it."

"I believe in the harmony of perfect proportion and the simple elegance of line, where design is graceful and sophisticated," says Eve. "I believe we make our own rules for the way we want to live and express ourselves, and the process of creation and design should be fun."

FANNY HAIM

BEFORE SHE MOVED TO MIAMI, FANNY HAIM SPENT a large portion of her creative training apprenticing under Colombian artist David Manzur, and exhibited in major galleries and museums in both Colombia and Washington, D.C. That invaluable training and years spent as a professional fine artist now allow Fanny to view her design practice through the eyes of a creative, and to paint a picture, define the spirit of the space, and write the story that will ultimately become the script for that particular project.

"The need to be creative fuels and sustains my practice, and my deep love for human interaction keeps me engaged and motivated," she says. "That creative thirst, coupled with passion and enthusiasm, builds trust, and that trust inevitably allows you to be the best version of yourself."

The licensed and registered interior designer studied fine arts at the University of Los Andes in Bogotá, Colombia, and later at the University of Miami, before heading up her award-winning design firm for the past three decades.

"I always say that design is not a self-service enterprise," Fanny says. "Unlike the fine artist, who creates for him or herself, a designer is bound to use their talent and creative vision to fulfill the needs and aspirations of others. It is a huge responsibility to be the creative steward."

"A great designer doesn't convince—a great designer seduces."

A capacity to listen and really delve into the "inner places" of her clients' psyches is something at which Fanny excels. She takes what she learns and crafts a concept that is reflective of those dreams and aspirations, often leading to a reaction of sheer astonishment at how well Fanny and her team "got them."

Observing everything, and not just what her clients provide, is how Fanny remains constantly inspired. Micro-moments in nature, light and shadow, organic rhythm and repetition—these all encourage reflection and spur creativity. Travel, the ultimate inspiration and one of Fanny's true passions, opens yet another portal for observation. Moments from every journey find their way back into Fanny's work, where they blend with the clients' goals.

"I do believe that without creative immersion and even playfulness, there is no platform," says Fanny. "I am an enemy of trends or 'colors of the year,' because they date the projects and keep them stuck in time. I get tremendous satisfaction in visiting a project from the past and still finding it exciting and relevant. But at its heart, the space always has to represent the user—it should not merely be a testament to the designer's talent." ›

The tension created by juxtaposing items of diverse provenance or time periods has always intrigued Fanny, who strives to create moments of unexpected ambiguity. Myriad textures in lieu of patterns complement monochromatic schemes, which Fanny personally favors as a way to remain classic and timeless. "I do like colors," she says, "but not all of them at once."

HILLARY LITTLEJOHN SCURTIS

HILLARY LITTLEJOHN SCURTIS NEVER ANTICIPATED THAT her business degree and art history classes from Southern Methodist University, as well as her experience in sales, teaching and working at an auction house would create the professional trajectory of her current career: interior designer. After renovating and decorating her own homes, Scurtis' friends and family took note and often asked her for advice and help with their own projects. It occurred to Hillary that she could parlay this into a career.

She launched Hillary Littlejohn Scurtis Design in Miami in 2005 and subsequently returned to school and earned her Interior Design Certificate from Parsons The New School in 2011. "You can never predict how your life is going to turn out," she says. "I feel like everything I have done, all these disparate experiences I've had, led me to where I am right now. It's truly something I enjoy. I don't consider it work."

Hillary's studio, HLS Design, focuses on high-end residential, with a few select commercial projects. She says her design style is a mix of old and new, and she carefully edits her designs, especially when it comes to the quality and quantity of light, to ensure interior spaces flow and properly interact with the outdoors. "I find a lot of inspiration from designers and architects in California, who work with the same natural elements as we do in Florida."

Hillary says for a design project to be a success, rooms must have an engaging narrative and easily transition from one space to the next. An important key to accomplishing this look and feel is creating an environment that's in harmony with the client's needs. "Every room should tell a story with a beginning, middle, and ending that is coherent and inspiring," she says.

HLS Design projects are primarily residential, but her most recent collaboration is a bit of a surprise. She's currently working with her husband, a real estate developer, on designing and building state-of-the-art storage facilities. Far from the typical gray, industrial-looking concrete blocks, Hillary says their storage units look like contemporary art museums, complete with street-level gallery space.

"Art museums and storage units actually have many of the same constraints, like security, lighting, human circulation, and height restrictions," she says. "We're taking something that is often a blight—some big, hulking building—and creating a facility that can make a community richer." ›

> "Every room should tell a story with a beginning, middle, and ending that is coherent and inspiring."

When she's not working, Hillary, who has three sons, loves to travel, especially when the trips incorporate food. In fact, she recently flew across the country to California to take a cooking class with noted chef and author Pamela Salzman. "Food is another discipline of art and can inspire the way we enjoy spaces," she says.

JENNIFER GARRIGUES

LOTS OF THINGS IN LIFE ARE MORE IMPORTANT than interior design, but to me it's everything," says Jennifer Garrigues. "I've always burned the candle at both ends and in the middle because I love every moment of it." Uniquely attuned to the finer points of design, she spent the early part of her career as a model, frequenting the fashion capitals of the world and soaking up all the inspiration they have to offer. She has traveled the globe many times over and has a deep reverence for fine design of all sorts.

Whether at home or abroad, Jennifer begins each project quite simply with a close look at who the residents are and who they want to be. Jennifer loves to translate intangible qualities into perfectly tailored living spaces that feel at once authentic, interesting, and elegant.

Jennifer works with everyone from first-time homeowners discovering their style to veteran homeowners refining their lifestyle, and she thoroughly enjoys the variety. Some clients love the showroom scene and accompanied shopping excursions where the possibilities abound, while others are perfectly content giving a nod of approval to whatever Jennifer designs. She meets them wherever they are with a knowing smile of encouragement and nudges them to the next level.

Her disarming personality is one of her greatest assets, easily melting away new clients' inhibitions. She once jetted over to Morocco to connect with an adventuresome couple for the first time; within a week, they had collaboratively designed nearly the entire residence and filled several shipping crates with handmade treasures.

Eschewing a signature style in favor of looks as diverse as her clientele, Jennifer explains that creative people can set their minds to most styles. Jennifer's love of history, art, architecture, fashion—and everything else that has anything to do with design—allows her to passionately delve into any style. She appreciates the cognitive and creative challenges of understanding a historically rooted style so well that she can flawlessly reinterpret it for the 21st century. She finds it thrilling to help clients bring home the essence of Italy or India or some other cherished destination in a way that makes sense in their North American residence. Her designs often make the residents look as well-traveled as they wish to be. Jennifer is a designer of great depth, so whatever the project, she immerses herself in the given stylistic context until she falls in love with it. Understandably, her portfolio covers the full spectrum of looks, and while each is unique, all have the scent of authenticity, whimsy, and an uninhibited zest for life.

A self-proclaimed eternal-optimist, Jennifer is not one to dwell on the many challenges of the interior design profession—from the interpersonal nuances and logistics of working with vendors around the world to the day-to-day management of seemingly millions of details and deadlines. She simply greets each surprise with a problem-solving mentality and gracefully designs her way through.›

"If you're a red and orange person, you're not going to be happy in grays and blues, no matter how delightfully sophisticated they look."

Some creative professionals are content with a job well done, content to see the fruits of their labor and soak up the praise lavished by their clients. Jennifer, however, wraps up each gorgeous installation with an internal review of what she has learned from the experience, what her clients have taught her, and how she'll guide them on their next adventure together. With all her heart, she believes that the process of design should be fun, if not entirely magical, and she sees to it that her clients feel the same.

JONATHAN PARKS

WITH THE BELIEF THAT THOUGHTFUL DESIGN CAN change the way people live, Jonathan Parks makes it his goal with each new project to elevate life's everyday rituals from mundane to noble, poignant, and even fun. The Amherst, New York, native starts his designs with a conversation and a pencil, listening as his clients convey their wishes—both known and as-yet unrealized—for the project.

"A major part of the job is having to discover everything a client wants to tell you," says Jonathan. "Clients often come to you for the remarkable but cannot communicate in those terms. It surprises people how important it is to simplify."

For more than 20 years, Jonathan has been developing his firm into a multidisciplinary practice focused on re-imagining residential design in Southwest Florida. The award-winning work has been recognized by the AIA and published broadly.

At the heart of each new undertaking is one simple goal: actually construct the work. The principal, who did his graduate architecture studies at the University of Pennsylvania, always remembers that truly memorable buildings are only as timeless as the thought that has been put into them, and therefore strives to continually trust and stay true to his instincts. Jonathan places importance not only on the tangible, such as volume and shape, but also on immaterial elements of transparency, light, and space.

"My work relates strongly to the craft of building and to the assemblage of spaces, typically from the inside out," he says. "But the secret to success is an awareness that what I do is a backdrop. People are more important than the space around them."

Though well-schooled in the history of his profession, Jonathan is careful not to let this extensive knowledge stifle his creativity. He seeks out inspiration that's visual and tactile, and a great deal of it often comes directly from nature.

"Frank Lloyd Wright once said that nature, above all else, was his most inspirational force," says Jonathan. "'Study nature, love nature, stay close to nature. It will never fail you,' he said. To date, I find nothing in my career that contradicts Mr. Wright's advice."

A self-proclaimed regionalist, Jonathan has found that truly examining a building or design's context allows him to consider solutions that are not preconceived. This approach also discourages the temptation to utilize ideas that are popular, but which may not be right for the area—an inclination that he recognizes all too often in younger designers. ›

> "The design process is rooted in reduction, but there is a recognition that life is quite beautiful in its messiness."

"If you tour any architecture school in the world, most of the student projects are amazing and better than what we live with day-to-day," Jonathan says. "The talent is spectacular and never-ending, so why are there so many bad buildings going up all the time? Graduates should have faith in their capabilities and carry that into their professional careers. The first mark of a truly great designer is to speak clearly with their own voice and not to copy others. The second mark is to actually construct what you are designing."

JUAN CARLOS ARCILA-DUQUE

IN ADDITION TO INTERIOR DESIGN, JUAN CARLOS Arcila-Duque sees his role as somewhat of an editor. From the beginning of each project, he is sure to engage in clear communication with his clients that, though it sometimes may feel painful or risky, is vital to ensure that everyone is on the same page when it comes to a room's or home's desired finished outcome.

"The world is full of images, and clients are exposed to a lot of great design lately," he says. "I do believe our job is to edit their dreams. After all, we are only designers, not magicians."

Those important conversations do the trick, it seems, because Juan Carlos has developed so many relationships with devoted clients that he is working on their children's homes now as well. The Miami-based designer, who originally hails from Colombia, established his first design studio in New York City in the early '90s. His projects now span the globe and include private residences, corporate offices, restaurants, and boutique hotels. But no matter how established a client may be, each project is approached with the same level of excitement as if it were the very first.

Finding inspiration in art and nature, as well as bohemian neighborhoods around the world—"In the past I've been called a minimalist-bohemian designer," he says—Juan Carlos approaches everything he does with the aim of keeping the world beautiful. He promotes the work of young artists, collecting and dealing photography while cycling it through his own home, which he calls his own personal art installation. He is so integrated into the local art scene that he even serves as co-chair of the Junior Committee for Art Basel Miami.

One thing you'll never see him selecting is plastic furniture, a scourge of bad taste that is at odds with the warm and simple, yet modern, aesthetics he champions. Ergonomic pieces that are comfortable as well as a complement to the room's overall design, however, are things he wishes he had insisted upon earlier in his career. The longevity of a piece plays another important role in Juan Carlos' designs: whenever he is able to reuse a family heirloom or re-imagine it in another way, he does.

"I think what surprises my clients is my ability to recycle," he says. "I love to reuse pieces that are part of the family history, as well my capacity to negotiate on their behalf. It is a compliment that I always get at the end of the project."›

> "The best ideas always happen in the first meeting—trust your instincts."

Working with a room's existing architecture is another specialty of his, as long as that architecture itself isn't beyond saving. Respecting a room's bones allows whatever design Juan Carlos dreams up to blend into, rather than compete against, the space, resulting in a harmonious finished product. "The client is always right as long as it is my way," he jokes.

JUAN POGGI

JUAN POGGI WILL BE THE FIRST TO TELL YOU THAT interior designers are not indispensable, and that life can carry on very well without them. But the founder and owner of Poggi Design will also tell you that each person's unique experience—and, in turn, their home—is much better off for having a designer serve as the interpreter of their wishes.

"We are an article of luxury," Juan says. "People can live without us. But it is very nice to live better thanks to design."

Comfort and luxury remain Juan's goals with each new space he designs, whether that's a condo in Miami, an apartment in Ibiza, or a home in Paris. That's because comfort and luxury are one in the same, Juan has found, and obtaining one should always lead to the other.

Juan is constantly on alert for the starting point of his next project, knowing that inspiration can be found in both the exotic and the everyday. It might be a color, a piece of furniture, something he spots on his many travels, or even a cartoon (a good source of color harmony, he has found); but whatever triggers his avalanche of ideas, it will always come back to his client.

Clean lines and uncluttered spaces are Juan's personal trademarks, and fall under the umbrella of his term "soft contemporary"—meaning comfort is always key, no matter how sleek the space. In the end, however, it all comes back to each of his client's unique wishes.

"I will raise the volume, but the basic melody always comes from the client," he says.

Often that symphony depends on awakening the senses: textures that slide from soft to rough, materials that vary between light and heavy, lines that alternate between static and dynamic. From there, Juan advances to a dance of ideas that includes pigments, dimensions, and the client's grounding vision to bring beautiful form to functional spaces.

Ideally, this entire process happens within six months or less, as he has found that for most people, the excitement that arrives so readily at the start of a new endeavor quickly dissipates. What was once a thrilling journey into self-exploration has become, sadly, a chore. Juan aspires to never let that happen for his clients, and chooses his team with care to ensure that the work is done with speed and always with the utmost attention to detail.›

"Expensive does not always mean the best."

"My work is a constant, personal search for better expressions for living interiors," says Poggi. "Evolution is a process of seeking, adapting, and, in many ways, the story of life itself. My purpose is to create deeply personal and peaceful homes."

JUDITH LIEGEOIS

GROWING UP IN NORTHERN NEW ZEALAND'S BAY OF Islands, "playing house" for Judith Liegeois meant drawing floorplans in the sand with a stick, dragging driftwood walls into place, and then decorating the spaces she had conjured up with seashells and kelp. At night, the tide would come in and wash it all away, so Judith would simply start all over again in the morning.

"Living in New Zealand instilled in me a strong connection to nature and a deep appreciation for organic materials," she says. "I love art, antiques, vintage items, beautiful textures, and textiles, and I love to mix exquisite, man-made things with natural items."

That admiration for elements that are both unusual and classic strongly informs Judith's design philosophy today, along with a unique sense of color, style, and placement; her keen eye for detail; and a deep desire to involve her clients in all aspects of the process. Collaboration between Judith, her team, and her clients is paramount—the experience is often referred to as a "roundtable," where rules do not apply and each member of the project can feel free to bring all manner of creative ideas to the arena.

In addition to interior design services that are always approached with fresh enthusiasm, Judith offers space planning, lighting, color study, upholstery, home styling, and furniture design. Oh, and her unofficial specialty: organization and cleaning.

"Often in a finished house, I will be the one that goes in and cleans—even after the cleaning staff. It is part of the finishing process for me," Judith says. "Even when I go back to visit a home I have finished, I start to put things in place where I think they should be. I plump the pillows, straighten the shades…most of my clients don't mind at all."

Having Judith's final touch is a highly sought-after reward for those seeking a space that's infused with plenty of comfort and style. Even those who do not engage her design services can obtain a little piece of her personality, as Judith also operates a gallery and showroom that's populated with a curated collection of home furnishings, lighting, curiosities, gifts, accent pieces, and artwork. It's a mix of classic, vintage, and contemporary sensibilities, and nearly all of the stock is sourced from Judith's extensive travels around the United States and abroad.

"I adore hunting for and finding treasures in antique stores and at estate sales," she says. "When I'm not working, you'll find me visiting great museums in New York, Paris, London, and elsewhere for inspiration." ›

> "Allow yourself to be intoxicated by the revelation and discovery of travel. Inspiration is everywhere."

Spaces that are elegant, refined, interesting, and unique: that's the end result when Judith is at the helm. And she will not rest until she's satisfied with the final iteration of a design, which always takes into consideration her clients' most personal wishes and preferences. Everything in a home should bring its occupants pleasures, whether that's through form, touch, color, or sentiment. "Integrity, consciousness, diligence, kindness, and a deep love for what I do," Judith says. "It is who I am."

KURT DANNWOLF
& LACHMEE CHIN

CREATIVE AND HARMONIOUS COLLABORATION IS THE driving force behind ODP Architecture & Design's success. Founded by Kurt Dannwolf and Ed O'Donnell, the firm is noted for its innovative, award-winning projects, ranging from luxury, high-rise mixed-use projects to expansive tropical island estates.

Initially the company focused mostly on architecture. But when Kurt and Ed decided to expand their business strategy to include interior design, they brought on Lachmee Chin in 2005 to spearhead this new direction.

"I enjoy the design process," Lachmee says. "I equate it to great cooking. It's about being in the moment and enjoying; once it is over you can still savor it and enjoy all the passion that went into it."

Over the years, Lachmee has developed a special working relationship with Kurt, who oversees architecture. Together, they have designed some of Florida's most dazzling and luxurious residences, including a 10,000-square-foot penthouse atop the 70-story Four Seasons Hotel and Residences in Miami.

This modern yet comfortable space is indicative of ODP's unique collaborative process. While both Lachmee and Kurt bring their own perspective and style, their differences complement each other and together they create cohesive, unified projects.

"We respect each other's work and opinions," says Lachmee. "When we start a project, we take it on holistically. From planning the proper spacing to selecting the right furniture and fabrics, we're always communicating and providing feedback."

"Lachmee is really good at taking my ideas about space and form and reinforcing them through her use of fabrics, stone, and other materials," adds Kurt. "It's that back-and-forth process that creates really fantastic spaces."

Initially Lachmee was unsure about working for an architectural firm. Based on her previous experience, Miami-area architects were a little too laid back and casual for her tastes. But Kurt spent much of his career in New York and brought a different kind of energy. He worked previously for Handel Architects, which designed the World Trade Center Memorial. While at Handel, Kurt spearheaded the company's Four Seasons Hotel and Residences, which brought him to Florida, where he founded ODP in 2003.

Currently, ODP Architecture has almost 10 million square feet of space under design and construction valued at just under $3 billion. This includes a 20,000-square-foot home in the Bahamas. "We're still in concept development, but we have a team of three architects and an interior designer working on this," says Kurt. "It's important for us that the interior designer's input regarding use of space and functionality is thought about from the beginning."

In addition to inspiring work, both Lachmee and Kurt enjoy having fun with their co-workers. Recently, Lachmee joined Kurt and some of the other guys from the office for an autocross competition, during which participants drove sports cars through a series of cones in a timed event. ›

"Simply put, I enjoy the design process. I equate it to great cooking. It's about being in the moment and enjoying; once it is over you can still savor it and enjoy all the passion that went into it."
Lachmee Chin

"With our kind of work, you use your brain constantly," says Lachmee. "During autocross, all you can think about is making sure you get through the course as fast as you can. It was a nice reprieve from the technical side of our jobs. In a weird way, it allowed us all to relax."

LAURA MARTZELL

THERE'S PERFECTION AND THERE'S SETTLING, AND Laura Martzell has always done everything she can to ensure she delivers the former. In the past, this has meant painting, installing wallpaper, sewing, cleaning, and even laying tile—you name it and the designer has probably done it, all in the quest for the best possible outcome for her clients.

"I'm always thinking of ways to improve on literally everything," she says. "The time I spend on plans, drawings… I have an obsession to deliver someone's desires with the best quality there is."

More than 42 years in the business has provided Laura with plenty of opportunities to chase perfection. Her designs have appeared not just throughout Florida, but also in Louisiana, Texas, Massachusetts, North Carolina, New York, Illinois, Colorado, Canada, and Washington, D.C. Along with lead designer and project manager Madelein Rodriguez, who joined the company in 2006, Laura cultivates partnerships with the best trades and resources in the business.

"I have always strived to listen very carefully, very thoughtfully, for what that person or family wants to achieve," says Laura. "Their vision is my job, and the reason they hired me is to make that dream come true."

> "Patience and trust in your design team will achieve your goal of a beautiful home."

Part of building that dream is discovering inspiration, and for that, Laura is constantly on the lookout. Whether she's walking the beach on Harbour Island in the Bahamas (her favorite vacation spot), going to a Broadway show in New York City, shopping the shoe department in Bergdorf's, strolling through Paris, or watching a classic movie, she's always keenly aware of the textures, hues, and architecture that surround her. Studying art and reading about different cultures is also illuminating, and even just driving through different neighborhoods often leads to noticing certain shades or colors that she'll mentally file away for use in future projects.

Amid all the conceptualization and inspiration-gathering, Laura's "planner" nature still shines through when it's time to undertake a home or office's transformation. Keeping everyone—from the tradespeople and the installers to even her clients —on track is something that at which she excels, though having a few more hours in a day would never hurt.

"Sometimes it's a challenge for everyone to understand the real process of a project," Laura says. "It's not like the TV shows. A day really is only 24 hours, and even I have trouble accepting that sometimes." ›

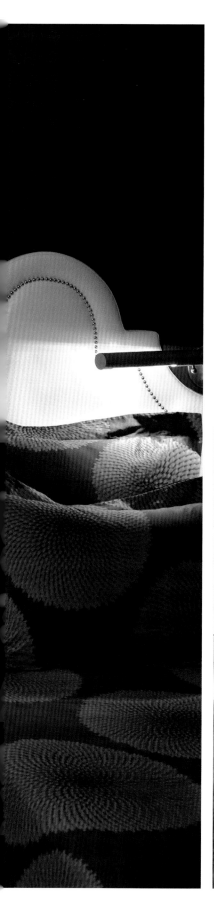

The consistently classic, clean lines that Laura produces, along with furniture and accessories that have been carefully selected to reflect each client's lifestyle and personality, make the end result more than worth it. Add in a process where frustration has been kept to a minimum, and it's no wonder that people often return to Laura Martzell Designs time and again. With each space she designs, Laura hopes that her clients are as happy in it as she is within her own home.

LEILI FATEMI

WHEN LEILI FATEMI'S AUNT WAS BUILDING A NEW house, she asked her niece for design advice — the unusual part was that, at the time, Leili was still a child. It was just one of the many indicators that Leili would grow up to be an accomplished, professional interior designer, with international experience and an impressive roster of credentials.

"I love what I do and always knew I wanted to be a designer," says Leili. "Now I create interiors that are not only visually appealing and functional but are fully executed design concepts that integrate artistic vision and resonate on a deeper level for my clients."

She has found that the greatest joy in her career is also the greatest challenge: Each project is different, and she never knows what to expect. Every client that she works with is unique, with a distinct set of wishes, wants, requirements, and dreams, and it's up to Leili to listen, understand, and then bring to life a design that exceeds even their wildest expectations. Her positive attitude and friendly manner invite people to open up to her, which is invaluable when it comes to building lifelong relationships with her clients.

Through her nearly two decades of professional experience, Leili has found that most people incorrectly assume that interior design is mostly about furniture choice. As a former graphic designer and avid admirer of all art forms, Leili sees the entire picture when putting together a room. Whenever possible she has a hand in the design of custom elements, from hand-selecting artwork to sketching furniture and accessories that will then be built to her exact specifications.

"To me, creating the best interior is not about stylish furnishings or adding attractive accessories to a room," she says. "It's more about the creative process and making the best use of the space through unique touches."

With an international background and a profound love of travel, Leili has enjoyed experiencing cultures, décor, and styles of living from all over the world. The ease with which she adapts to new situations also means she has a keen talent for quickly understanding both her clients and their space.

"Space itself speaks to me," says Leili. "The prospect of a blank canvas guides me to new and fresh ideas." ›

> "Life is too short to make your interiors too complicated."

Sometimes it is an aspect of a client's personality that ends up informing the colors and textures of a design, while in other instances the driving force might be a room's specific requirement. Either way, it is up to Leili to determine through careful listening not only what might work, but what will surely wow her clients at the final reveal. —"It's always my goal that the end result is not something they like," she says, "but something that they love."

MARGARITA & CRISTINA COURTNEY

THE MOTHER-AND-DAUGHTER TEAM OF MARGARITA and Cristina Courtney have a unique and easy bond, often finishing each other's sentences and laughing at the same inside jokes. It's a chemistry that has served them well as the co-owners of Margaux Interiors, a full-service design and renovation firm in Miami that offers its clients fine art, stylish furniture, and accessories from around the world.

In addition to a supportive relationship, the two also share a love of travel and beautiful things, which is evident in their many luxury residential design projects. "Cristina and I complement each other," says Margarita. "We don't have the same tastes, but we still gel nicely. Our design ideas never seem to be too far apart."

The two have traveled all over the world together, including recent trips to India, Thailand, Singapore, Indonesia, Spain, Milan, Lake Como, and Rome. These exotic experiences and adventures often inform their design styles and choices. "Everywhere we go I'm on the lookout for new, interesting, and beautiful things," says Margarita. "They become a part of your subconscious. Miami is very multicultural with a lot of different influences, and we can create sophisticated styles that fit our clients very well."

Born in Puerto Rico, Margarita moved to Miami when she was 5, then returned to Puerto Rico as a young teenager. After she got married—she recently celebrated her 50th anniversary—she came back to Miami, where Cristina was born.

Margarita started Margaux Interiors in 1988. Growing up, Cristina often worked at her mother's business during summer breaks from high school and college. After she graduated college she moved to New York City where she worked in the furniture and design industry. But by this time Margaux Interiors was really taking off, and after a few years Cristina returned to Miami to join the family business in 2000.

Today, Cristina, who now has two kids of her own, says Margaux Interiors is not only a thriving business but an integral part of the family. Employees bring their pets to work and she often hosts her kids' birthday parties at the store. "It's just a fun, family-friendly environment," says Cristina.

While the two sometimes work independently on projects, they usually work as a team. Whoever gels with the client better typically takes the lead. The duo pride themselves on creating beautiful, harmonious spaces that reflect the personality of each client. They accomplish this by discussing important lifestyle details with clients and being meticulous, organized, and detail-oriented. "The end product may look beautiful, creative, and fun, but the process is complicated. We're perfectionists and clients expect a lot from us," says Cristina. ›

"Everywhere we go I'm on the lookout for new, interesting, and beautiful things. They become a part of your subconscious."

"We're here to please people, and people are not always easy to please," adds Margarita. "So it's very satisfying when you create something beautiful and the customer loves it."

PAMELA IANNACIO

NOT TOO MANY PEOPLE CAN SAY THEY WORKED AT a pencil company. But it was one of Pamela Iannacio's first jobs, and the unlikely experience helped stoke her creativity and pave the way for her to launch Addison & Company Interiors, a full-service design firm in Tampa.

After earning a degree in developmental research and design from Briarcliffe College in New York, Pamela worked for a number of years in the fashion industry as a couture buyer for Saks Fifth Avenue, honing her design skills. Several years later, she returned home to Nashville to work for Empire Berol Company as Creative Design Director, which provide another platform for her creativity.

But Pamela's aspirations went beyond pencil design. She would go on to own her own wedding and event-planning business, and 1994 she opened the first Vera Wang Bridal Salon outside of New York. Four years later, Pamela and her family relocated to Tampa, Florida. Following the remodeling and design of their 1928 home, Pamela discovered her true passion and embarked on her new career.

"People started asking me to design their homes, and I knew that's what my passion was," she says

After working for several years with another designer, she opened Addison & Company Interiors in 2005.

"We're a full service design firm ," she says. "We assist our client in every element of the design process, from architecture and construction to the selection and installation of furniture, drapery, and art. The company also offers added concierge services to help coordinate moves, including unpacking and reorganizing all the family's belongings.

"When my clients walk into their new home, everything is ready," she says. "It's like the icing on top of the cake."

Pamela says most of her designs are "modern eclectic," and she takes pride in the fact that her projects are not only aesthetically pleasing, but also comfortable and functional. In recent years, her business has evolved from doing small projects to larger design projects–typically homes between 5,000 to 10,000 square feet—as well as commercial office space. And the scope of her business goes beyond Tampa, as she also designs homes in New York and Palm Beach. As part of her design process, Pamela often meets with the architects, general contractors and trades on design and construction issues, to ensure every detail of the project is flawless. ›

"I love what I do," she says. "When I'm working with a client, I listen and ask a lot of questions, and together we create a sanctuary that reflects who they are and what they're all about."

"I love what I do," Pamela says. "When I'm working with a client, I listen to what the client is telling me, what their thoughts are, and what their vision is. There is nothing more personal than a client's home. I'm constantly asking questions and suggesting ideas. Together, we create a sanctuary that reflects who they are, how they want to live, and what they're all about."

PHIL KEAN

ARCHITECT, CERTIFIED RESIDENTIAL CONTRACTOR, AND licensed interior designer Phil Kean adopts an "all under one roof" mentality with his firm, Phil Kean Design Group, because it lets him be involved each step of the way. And that's important to Kean, who prioritizes a seamless client experience. By offering everything from lot procurement to architectural design, local construction, finish selection, and furniture installation, the end result is a cohesive project.

"The ability to bring my architecture and construction experience into the design is invaluable," says Kean. "Great design starts with great architecture."

The son of a contractor, Kean knew since age 11 that architecture would be his future. He studied at Harvard University and Washington University, earning master's degrees in both architecture and business administration. But for all his credentials — and they are many — it's Kean's ability to extract and immediately translate a client's vision during the initial meeting that proves his natural talent.

Architectural style, unique lifestyle needs, and budget are all considered when embarking on a new project, as well as the opportunity to incorporate green practices into the design and construction process. One of the most experienced green builders in Central Florida, Phil Kean Design Group has achieved USGBC LEED-H Platinum, NAHB Green Emerald, FGBC Platinum, and Energy Star certifications.

"Utilizing green building methods means we are creating homes with extended life spans, less maintenance, and materials that can be recycled at the end of use," he says.

This includes designing and constructing homes that use energy, water, and materials efficiently; have a reduced impact on their physical environment; and promote a healthy indoor environment. Kean encourages a "never say no" approach, welcoming the chance to evolve a design if it means perfecting an aesthetic or function, or exceeding a client's expectations. From the smallest detail to the grandest, Kean and his group are designing for a better quality of life.

One of Kean's most distinctive style signatures is blurring the line between inside and out. Walls of glass that open to extensive indoor-outdoor living spaces are a hallmark, and complement the clean lines that Kean himself favors.

"I appreciate great design for both its beauty and function," he says. "My philosophy is to look at the classics and update them for today's style of living, then surround it all in art." ›

"Great design is intuitive, practical, and timeless."

Though well known for this contemporary and modern works, Kean is passionate about all styles of architecture. Other projects include homes that range from Spanish Mediterranean to French Country, Colonial to Traditional. The reach of Phil Kean Design Group is wide-ranging as well, extending not only across the United States but into the Bahamas, Canada, Spain, and Ghana.

An accomplished runner, Kean travels the country participating in marathons — and picking up inspiration in each city.

ROBERT BROWN & TODD DAVIS

IT WAS THE MOST FORTUITOUS DINNER PARTY OF TODD Davis' and Rob Brown's lives. The two had recently launched Brown Davis Interiors out of an expansive house they bought and designed in Washington, D.C.'s historic Georgetown neighborhood. As fate would have it, their neighbor was Susan Mary Alsop, a celebrated Washington socialite. Shortly after moving in to their house, Alsop invited them over for a dinner party.

Already electrified by the idea of rubbing elbows with Washington's elite, Rob was stunned when Aslop sat him between Paige Rense, who at the time was editor of Architectural Digest, and British ambassador Sir Christopher Meyer and Lady Catherine. "It was surreal," says Rob.

It got better. During the course of the dinner party, Lady Catherine asked Rob and Todd to design the British Embassy. Rense overheard the conversation and asked the two designers if she could look at their house next door.

"We left the table between dinner and desert and took her on a tour of the house," says Rob." She said she'd love to photograph it for the magazine. Todd and I just kind of looked at each other and said, 'OK.'"

Not only did Rense publish a feature on their house, she followed that up with a feature of their British Embassy design project. While Rob and Todd were designing the British Embassy, the ambassador invited them to parties with politicians, celebrities and movie stars. It was during one of these parties that the business partners met Bill and Hillary Clinton.

"Hillary loved how we had taken the embassy, which has very big, formal, imposing rooms, and made them warm, cozy, and inviting," says Todd.

The pair ended up designing two residences for the Clintons, including their home in Chappaqua, New York, as well Hillary's senate office. "They hired us as experts, and 99 times out of 100 went along with what we suggested," says Rob. "They were decisive, involved and wonderful to work with."

But by this time, in the early 2000s, the two began to feel constrained by the Washington market. Looking to expand, they opened a second office in Miami, where the company is now based.

Today, the pair work on an eclectic mix of traditional and modern projects, often integrating into their designs the area's saturated hues, tropical landscapes and sensual vitality. Rob stresses that their approach to design incorporates form, function and architecture.

"If we're building from scratch, we apply all the principles of fine architecture so that rooms look beautiful without a stick of furniture in them," he says.

"A great deal of intellectual thought and time go into a good design," adds Todd. "The project not only has to look good, but also function properly, so it naturally attracts people and makes them feel welcome."

After nearly 25 years of operating Brown Davis Interiors, Rob and Todd say they've never felt more inspired as they continue to design major projects in Miami, Washington, D.C., and other major markets like New York and Los Angeles. ›

"This is a remarkable industry where we get to conceptualize a project and a few years later we've literally changed the face of the earth by creating something new."
Rob Brown

"This is a remarkable industry where we get to conceptualize a project and a few years later we've literally change the face of the earth by creating something new," says Rob. "We are so enjoying being seasoned in our careers. The creative juices flow and it feels limitless in terms of our ideas and dreams."

ALEXANDER McQUEEN EVOLUTION

MARILYN MONROE AND THE CAMERA

ROBERT RIONDA

ROBERT RIONDA USED TO THINK HE WAS HAVING A design-identity crisis, because—try as he might—he couldn't trace a signature style through his work. But then he realized that his love of so many looks and his ability to become an expert at any historical notion or trending idea is a gift to the homeowners he works with, and to himself. Because he freely explores the full spectrum of design, he always feels invigorated, his projects always look fresh. With each home, Robert delves deeply into the lives and personalities of the owners to help them discover, develop, or fine-tune their own personal style. "More and more, people are looking for designs that nobody has seen, familiar looks presented in creative new ways," he says. "That's a designer's dream."

Robert travels the world with his clients and on their behalf, acquiring just the right furnishings, finishes, and works of art for each installation. A true aesthete, he loves to learn about the creative process of artists and artisans, appreciating so deeply their methods and motivations. Art plays a key role in all of his interiors. Helping experienced collectors complement their collections has its joys, yet Robert finds that there is something magical about working with younger patrons who

haven't a clue where to begin. He exposes them to as many artists, genres, and mediums as he can, instructing them to simply react to what they see and leave the details of scale, color, and placement analysis to him. "Don't worry about making mistakes," he always advises. "Don't worry about liking something that might not work in this house. Be open. Be confident. Communicate everything. I can make sense of it." When homeowners truly give themselves to the creative process and embark on a journey of self-discovery, they often end up with a different home than they expected, in good way.

Whether in one of the world's design capitals or someplace remote and exotic, Robert is always on the go, enjoying life, seeking inspiration, and finding the perfect pieces for his projects. Robert never stops working because his work is fun. He has the best job on the planet, in fact, and he fully appreciates it because his career path once looked so different. Before joining his mother in the design industry, Robert spent a decade working as a lawyer, and the analytical skills he developed have proven especially beneficial to his design clients. ›

"Only acquire art that you absolutely love. If you over-think the investment, you'll get lost in the shuffle."

Robert is gifted at not only design but also synthesizing vast quantities of information, negotiating with vendors, and accounting for multimillion-dollar budgets down to the last throw pillow, not to mention mediating conversations between husbands and wives whose ideas are sometimes—shall we say—disparate. The people are often the most challenging part of design, yet they are also Robert's favorite part. The psychology of design is as important as any combination of the stylistic elements in his repertoire.

ROBERT ZEMNICKIS

ROBERT ZEMNICKIS WAS TRAVELING FROM HIS NATIVE Canada to New York when he decided to visit Miami. He never left. The city's sunny weather, outdoor lifestyle and vibrant architecture all appealed to Robert, who has an interior design degree from Dawson College in Quebec.

"I had always been fascinated with architecture and had a good aptitude for visualizing things in three dimensions," says Robert. "But as I got older, architecture appealed to me less, and I really fell in love with interior design."

After settling in Miami, Robert worked for a few other designers but always knew he wanted to branch out on his own. "I was doing designs for other people and not getting a lot of acknowledgement or much money," he says. "I was ready for a change."

Robert launched Nuhouse Furniture + Design in 1995, an international, full-service design studio. He specializes in high-end interiors, commercial, hospitality, marine, residential and bespoke furniture and cabinetry.

"I have a fully integrated style," he says. "While some designers are very decorative, I'm more of an architectural designer. It's all about integrating the architecture to support the end design, materials, finishes and patterns. It's fully custom."

> "It's an amazing moment when I begin to turn a concept into something tangible and the client starts to see how it will all come together. They can now see how they fit into the space. That's the real fun part of my job."

Working mostly with new construction projects, Robert uses his design style to create engaging environments that reflect the personalities of the people who live within them. "That's where I find my inspiration," he says. "It's the synergy of the client, the project itself, and the architectural base. I'm making a 3-D representation of who the clients are. That's key to a successful project."

Robert says it's also key to focus on the details. He goes into each project with a keen eye for spacing, furniture, textures and materials—as well as what to edit out of a space. "Everything has to work together in order for a space to flow and be consistent," he says. And with so many people being inundated with design TV shows nowadays, Robert says it's important to gain a client's trust and steer them in the right direction, which often means preventing them from jumping on the latest fad or misguided approach.

In fact, gaining a client's trust and getting a sense of who they are is a key building block to any design project, Robert says. Armed with this nuanced information, Robert is able to create strong and meaningful connections between the user and the space. But sometimes this process can be challenging, especially if the client resists giving up control or isn't open to new ideas and concepts.›

"It can be frustrating, but my job is to bring something new to the table and help keep the client focused," he says. "They may not even be aware of what they need or want, and you have to guide them through dialogue and feedback. It's an amazing moment when I begin to turn a concept into something tangible and the client starts to see how it will all come together. They can now see how they fit into the space. That's the real fun part of my job."

SANDRA DIAZ-VELASCO

AS A CHILD, SANDRA DIAZ-VELASCO HAD AN INNATE passion for all mediums of artistic expression. She was constantly playing with colors, shapes, materials, and light, either creating something new or trying to fix things that—in her mind, anyway—needed improvement. Now that innate curiosity and artistic way of looking at the world is the backbone of her architecture and interior design firm, which she founded in 2008.

"We call ourselves a 'design boutique' primarily because of the high priority we place on attentive care and personalization," she says. "Whether it's hand sketches or computer imagery, I believe in an open, engaging, and fluid design process."

Sandra spent her childhood at her grandfather's master carpentry workshop in Colombia, being constantly influenced and inspired by his work. "I knew from then that I wanted to influence my surroundings in a more tangible way," she says.

Architecture and design became her creative outlet, first as an architect for the Colombian firm Coomeva, then as a project designer for the avant-garde Dean Lewis Architecture and as a principal project architect at the award-winning Taylor & Taylor Partnership on Miami Beach.

Now that 20 years of formal training and experience allows Sandra and her team to artfully integrate architecture, interior architecture, finishes, art, and furnishings in a way that is neither formulaic or predictable.

"As an architect, I see the bigger picture, ensuring quality work and efficient project management. As an interior designer, I see details that the owners are going to appreciate and interact with on a daily basis."

"We are grounded in both an artistic approach and a commitment to craftsmanship and innovation," says Sandra. "I like to create fresh looks with classic elements, using styles from timeless eras rather than trendy moments."

Timelessness is important not only for style and color choices, but as a part of the project's very foundation. Many of the projects that Sandra works on are not only residential, but also for commercial clients, developers, and domestic and foreign investors in Florida, Latin America, and the Caribbean. One of the firm's commercial projects was even presented with a "Keeping the City Beautiful" award from the city of Doral.

It's not unusual for inspiration to strike when it's least expected, since Sandra is constantly thinking about solutions and design elements. Often nature provides the nudge toward the next great idea, with color palettes coming together from an unusual flower or the way the sky looks as the sun is setting.

With that in mind, selecting elements that will withstand fads while truly expressing the client's desired look and feel is imperative. But so is function, meaning that even if a piece is absolutely gorgeous but will not work in the space, it's out.

"Editing is crucial—you have to keep in mind that the overall effect is more than the sum of its parts," says Sandra. "Sometimes you have to 'kill your darlings' to make the project shine as a whole." ›

And that takes trust from the client: trust in the firm's extensive research, years of experience, and high levels of expertise, all of which result in decisions that are guaranteed to last in the best and most beautiful way possible. "Architects see the bigger picture, ensuring quality work and efficient project management. Interior designers see details, the ones that the owners are going to appreciate and interact with on a daily basis," Sandra says. "It's important to understand both."

Photographs by Kris Tamburello

SAM ROBIN

FOR SAM ROBIN, ROOMS NEED TO BE CASUALLY elegant with a touch of sophistication and a bit of intellectual clutter. Clean lines and collectible pieces create spaces that are timeless and remembered.

With a desire to custom tailor their client's projects to their required needs, Sam Robin Design delivers specialized interiors with attention to detail and quality. Creating a unique and individual narrative for each project is key to her firm's ability to successfully weave a fluid consistency of design and concept throughout the installations. The firm is known for the stylish, modern designs it creates for prestigious clients, as well as the custom furniture and accessories it procures for both commercial and residential jobs.

Based in Miami, Florida, Sam has completed projects around the world, including airplanes for the Royal Air Wing of Dubai; chalets in Gstaad; and residences in London, Monaco, New York, L.A., and Chicago, to name a few. She designed 15 stores for Gianni Versace, as well as several hotel projects that include the Delano South Beach and the flagship South Beach hotel for Portugal's Pestana Group.

Inspired by great art and architecture, Sam never tires of exploring new venues of design or the incredible beauty of nature.

"I've spent my life immersed in design and product," she says. "I'm a visual listener with a big imagination, and no matter what style the client is trying to achieve I'm always searching for just the right elements to create that specific mood. In the end, it is the subtle details of a space that create the energy that inspires us, that comforts us, that heals us."

Sam's own home reflects her passions. Being a Bohemian at heart, her interiors are "red wine-friendly," with shelves full of memories and great food in the kitchen.

Never afraid to get her hands dirty, Sam actively participates in her installations, which assures perfection down to the smallest detail. Creating bespoke pieces for her interiors allows for her signature style to shine through, and she has established a beautiful line of furniture and accessories under Robicara, the brand she has created with her partner Francesco Caracciolo di Marano.›

"You need to be relevant to be a great designer."

"Design is definitely a process," Sam says, "and in my next life I'm absolutely requesting a magic wand." Although the transformation of spaces from concept to reality can be arduous at times, the end product and the energy it creates are well worth the wait. Sam and her team work to ensure that the process is a pleasant one for her clients. She enjoys the relationship that evolves and is always striving to surpass their expectations.

SARAH ZOHAR

PROJECTS THAT SARAH ZOHAR DESIGNS OFTEN HAVE a touch of glam to them, but the designer has never been afraid to do the less glamorous parts of a project herself. Her father was a builder, and she grew up immersed in the ins and outs of construction. This knowledge has proven immensely valuable now that she has her own firm, which offers full design-build services as well as more turnkey options.

"Having construction development experience gives me a leg up on most designers who don't want to get dirty, let alone fully understand what it takes to build out a project," says Sarah. "It surprises people when I go onsite and work with the general contractors and workers in order to make sure that every project goes as smoothly as possible."

A big part of that smoothness starts before anyone ever even picks up a tool. Sarah begins each project by listening, which in turn allows her to intimately connect to her clients and ultimately understand their needs and wants. Then the process of exploration and experimentation can begin.

"It is my job as a designer to put all the pieces together to complete their story within the final design," she says.

Always one to stay on top of the latest innovations, Sarah delights in pushing the envelope with her designs. There are no limits where concepts and ideas are concerned, and it's the ability to offer less traditional solutions that keeps Sarah and her team at the forefront of design.

"I love to use the latest fabrics, textures, finishes, and techniques from around the world, so I constantly challenge myself to push what we are able to do as a company," she says. "Constantly tapping into inspiration, creativity, and resourcefulness means you must also be able to constantly push the limits of design concepts and ideas."

Part of how Sarah maintains this continuous discovery is by cultivating relationships with other designers. She often hosts roundtable meetings where the latest techniques and best practices are discussed, and each designer can then use that collaborative knowledge in his or her own work.

Always on the lookout for new ideas, Sarah often turns to nature and her travels when she is seeking inspiration. She appreciates different forms and styles of architecture and design while visiting far-flung locales, but also taps into the serenity of raw nature found on a quiet beach or at a lake surrounded by mountains.

"I'm able to reconnect with myself and my thoughts in those kinds of settings," she says. "When I have time for myself I spend it with my kids, doing outdoor activities and connecting with nature." ›

"Just as each song has its own melody and every book has its own story, so does each design."

But in her own home, Sarah's love of family and entertaining is reflected in the design. I have an open concept kitchen overlooking the den, with an oversize sectional that can seat over 20 adults," she says. "This design allows me to host incredible parties and events, where all of my family and guests can eat food in the kitchen and nearby den while catching up and enjoying each other."

SHARRON LANNAN

NO MATTER WHERE SHE'S TRAVELING—NEW YORK, London, Paris, or Madrid—Sharron Lannan always has a notebook with her so she can sketch and jot down ideas for future projects.

"I am constantly inspired and awestruck in every city I visit," she says. "I find design inspiration everywhere: in my hotel room, a store, even restaurants. The creative juices never stop flowing when I am traveling."

Having grown up in a home where creativity was encouraged, Sharron developed a habit of spotting potential wherever she looked. Immersed in the California art scene by her parents, Sharron also learned early to differentiate between what was timeless and what was simply "of the moment," and today she applies that knowledge to the homes she designs.

When undertaking a new project, Sharron always pauses to consider if the grounding elements, such as flooring, cabinets, and significant furniture, pass the timelessness test.

"I think to myself, 'will this be a floor I would want to walk over 10 years from now? Will this be a color that has longevity? Is this trendy, or is this forever?'" she asks. "I purchased a Roche Bobois couch 14 years ago and it

"You have the rest of your life to invest in furniture and art; there is no need to rush that process."

remains relevant; it has found its place in seven moves. I have never tired of it."

Discovering exactly the right piece is another of Sharron's tenets of design. She is careful not to adhere to a single furniture designer, lest the rooms look like they came from a catalog, and does not adhere to a singular style or period. Her personal taste skews modern, but she is always ready to blend in eclectic or even antique pieces if they will help tie the room together. The result is that each project is markedly different, because each homeowner Sharron works with is unique.

One thing that remains, however, is Sharron's practice of billing a flat rate rather than a design fee. That inspires trust, she believes, because then homeowners know that she is selecting pieces for their merit rather than the commission she might receive. Creative problem solving and a practical approach have allowed her to work with an array of tastes and within a variety of budgets, and she welcomes each challenge.

Part of Sharron's success has been due to the people she chooses to work with, from architects who show mutual respect to general contractors who are as invested in completing the owners' dreams as she is. Egos, she points out, are never an asset. ›

At its core, each home Sharron designs is meant to reflect the people who live in it and show their personalities. "I feel the spaces I create look carefully curated by an artistic eye," she says, "with a combination of furniture from different periods, art in a variety of mediums and from a range of eras, and small collectors' items that personalize the spaces and tell a story of its inhabitants. At the end of the day, they are the ones who are going to live in the space."

SUSAN LOVELACE

CHASING AFTER HER DREAM, SUSAN LOVELACE TOOK a big gamble to launch her interior design company. Initially, the plan was for her and a friend to partner on the business venture. But when the friend backed out, Susan forged ahead and bought a sizeable piece of property in Miramar Beach.

"It was a leap of faith," she says. "I was young and fearless and went for it. My husband thought I was crazy, but he believed in me." Together, they built a 28,000-square-foot facility, including a 12,000-square-foot showroom. It became Susan's haven and creative workspace. Today, 23 years later, it's the base of operations for Lovelace Interiors, which employs about 20 people, over 10 designers. Moreover, Susan's husband, an attorney, and son, a realtor, also work out of the building.

"There's been some ups and downs, but it's worked out great for all of us," she says.

Susan says her business exemplifies her dedication to the principles and elements of good design. With projects all across the country, her team is skilled at interpreting the elements of each client's personal lifestyle and creating a classic, timeless design that makes them feel at home. Over the years, Susan's work has been published in some of the industry's most prestigious publications, including Architectural Digest, Southern Living and Coastal Living.

Blessed with two artistic parents, Susan grew up in a creative and inspiring environment. She began to really hone her design style while studying art history and fashion design in college. For a while she worked as an interior decorator for a builder, and then returned to school and completed an interior design program at Mississippi College.

Shortly after that she launched Lovelace Interiors in Miramar Beach. "We were like pioneers," she says. "This used to be a sleepy little fishing village, and everything had that typical beach condo look, with lots of peach colors and white wicker."

Susan craved a more sophisticated look—similar to Palm Beach or St. Augustine—and, through a process of trial and error, began developing her elegant yet relaxed signature style, including bleached floors, antiques, and casual fabrics that can still withstand the Florida sun.

Susan focuses mostly on high-end residential work, although she does do the occasional commercial project, including chef Emeril Lagasse's new restaurant in Miramar Beach's vibrant outdoor mall, Grand Boulevard.

Susan explains that she's cousins with Lagasse's wife, Alden. When she and her husband were looking to downsize, they swapped their sizeable 8,000-square-foot home near Destin for Lagasse's smaller residence. Susan then designed the home for the celebrity chef and his wife, incorporating a soothing, creamy white color scheme, custom-made furniture and contemporary pieces, along with painted French and Italian antiques and bejeweled Empire chandeliers. The home was featured in Veranda magazine both when Susan owned it and after she completed the design for Lagasse.

For Lagasse's new restaurant, Emeril's Coastal Italian, Susan is using an earthy mix of textures to create a casual, coastal feeling, with elegant and sophisticated touches. ›

"You can be talented and creative and organized, but you also have to have people skills. If you can't engage the client and the phone isn't ringing, then you're never going to make it."

Looking back over her decades-spanning career, Susan says her success is as much about her design capabilities as it is her business acumen. "You can be talented and creative and organized, but you also have to have people skills. If you can't engage the client and the phone isn't ringing, then you're never going to make it."

WHITNEY BLOOM

WHEN WHITNEY BLOOM MAKES A PLAN FOR HER DAY, she packs enough in to where people assume she's mapping out a schedule for three days. That's because the enthusiastic designer is so deeply involved in her chosen career path that there simply aren't enough hours in a typical day to contain all the ideas she has when working on a project.

"What makes me a fabulous designer? Great ideas. And the secret to my success? You guessed it: more ideas," says Whitney. "I have no shortage of great ideas—one leads to another and another, and there's no end. I often go for 20 hours straight trying to fit in all the things I want to do, because I love it."

Before moving to Florida, Whitney worked in broadcast news in New York City, soaking up the museums and Broadway theater while studying at the New York School of Interior Design on the side. Now she directs her passion toward creating beautiful spaces in the magnificent environment of Miami, working on both residential and commercial projects for the Sunshine State.

In addition to creating great spaces in tandem with her clients, to whom she devotes an extraordinary amount of time listening, Whitney directs her energy toward mastering the ever-changing technological aspect of her career, knowing that having a firm handle on the wave of the future is a valuable investment.

"The endless amount of technological skills required today are some of the most challenging parts of being a designer," she says. "It's very cool, but very time consuming."

But nothing can replace good, old-fashioned commitment to an idea. Whitney once spent the better part of two days hand-placing carpet tiles in a specific pattern, because the 2,500-square-foot room's design all but demanded it. To find a designer who will not only strategize, but also participate in all the stages of design and execution is beyond valuable.

"The mark of a great designer is getting something right, whatever it is," says Whitney. "The amount of time that goes into planning something is astounding. A great designer can achieve whatever style the client wants only with the added bonus of a custom flair."

To help achieve these one-of-a-kind designs, Whitney seeks out beautiful elements of nature and colors, and travels whenever possible, having hit Japan, Africa, and the Caribbean, in addition to her beloved New York, to gather inspiration for possible future projects. Though her overall style may be timeless, Whitney relies on the unique pieces and inspiration she acquires while globetrotting to add that something extra to her contemporary and timeless designs.›

"Always try to make the world you live in beautiful."

But for all Whitney's international travel, few places provide the stability and comfort of home. An open kitchen in her private abode is ideal for entertaining family and friends, while massive views in the bedroom make it feel as if you can see right into the next day. "My home is definitely a place where fun and relaxation can happen," she says. "I'm often reminded of what I love the most about my job, and it's all the people I meet: clients, designers, painters, carpenters, residents—together they all make my day and I find time to get to know everyone at least a little bit. That's the compassion that the world is sorely in need of."

"We shape our homes
and then our homes shape us."

Winston Churchill

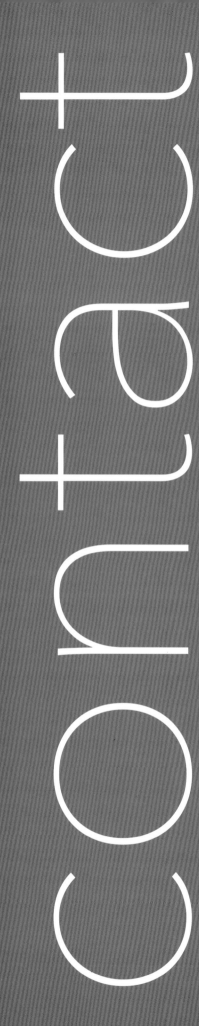

contact

Laura Martzell Designs | Photograph by Troy Campbell Studio

special thanks

We would like to thank all the photographers who contributed to this book.

Barry Fitzgerald
barryfitzgerald.com

Barry Grossman
grossmanphoto.com

Carlos Domenech Photography
domenechphoto.com

Claudia Uribe Touri Photography
claudiauribe.com

Colleen Duffley Productions
colleenduffleyphotography.com

Gavin Doran
gavindoran.com

John Sciarrino, Giovanni Photography
giophoto.com

Juan Pablo Estupinan

Ken Hayden Photography
kenhayden.com

Kris Tamburello
kristamburello.com

Lori E. Hamilton Photography
lorihamiltonphoto.com

Mark Roskams Photography
markroskams.com

Moris Moreno Photography
morismoreno.com

Native House Photography
nativehousephotography.com

Paul Stoppi
stoppi.net

Rocky Gonet Photography
rockygonetphotography.com

Ron Rosenzweig
rons-prophoto.com

Ryan Gamma Photography
ryangammaphotography.com

Sarah Yunker Photography
sarahyunker.com

Stephen Allen Photography
sallenphoto.com

Troy Campbell Studio
troycampbellstudio.com

Uneek Photography
uneekluxurytours.com

Zack Smith Photography
zacksmith.com

Poggi Design | Photograph by Carlos Domenech Photography

HLS Interior Design | Photograph by Mark Roskams Photography